Migrating Animals

Penguins

B.J. Best

New York

Published in 2017 by Cavendish Square Publishing, LLC
243 5th Avenue, Suite 136, New York, NY 10016

Copyright © 2017 by Cavendish Square Publishing, LLC

First Edition

No part of this publication may be reproduced, stored in a retrieval system, or transmitted in any form or by any means—electronic, mechanical, photocopying, recording, or otherwise—without the prior permission of the copyright owner. Request for permission should be addressed to Permissions, Cavendish Square Publishing, 243 5th Avenue, Suite 136, New York, NY 10016. Tel (877) 980-4450; fax (877) 980-4454.

Website: cavendishsq.com

This publication represents the opinions and views of the author based on his or her personal experience, knowledge, and research. The information in this book serves as a general guide only. The author and publisher have used their best efforts in preparing this book and disclaim liability rising directly or indirectly from the use and application of this book.

CPSIA Compliance Information: Batch #CW17CSQ

All websites were available and accurate when this book was sent to press.

Library of Congress Cataloging-in-Publication Data

Names: Best, B.J.
Title: Penguins / B.J. Best.
Description: New York : Cavendish Square Publishing, 2017. | Series: Migrating animals | Includes index.
Identifiers: ISBN 9781502621061 (pbk.) | ISBN 9781502621085 (library bound) | ISBN 9781502621078 (6 pack) | ISBN 9781502621092 (ebook)
Subjects: LCSH: Penguins--Juvenile literature.
Classification: LCC QL696.S473 B4475 2017 | DDC 598.47--dc23

Editorial Director: David McNamara
Copy Editor: Nathan Heidelberger
Associate Art Director: Amy Greenan
Designer: Alan Sliwinski
Production Coordinator: Karol Szymczuk
Photo Research: J8 Media

The photographs in this book are used by permission and through the courtesy of: Cover MZPHOTO.CZ/Shutterstock.com; p. 5 Brian Maudsley/Shutterstock.com; p. 7 MikeCardUK/iStockphoto.com; p. 9 Education Images/UIG/Getty Images; p. 11 Volt Collection/Shutterstock.com; p. 13 Paul Souders/Getty Images; p. 15 Frans Lanting/Mint Images/Getty Images; p. 17 Frederique Olivier/Hedgehog House/Getty Images; p. 19 Martin Ruegner/Getty Images; p. 21 Jan Vermeer/Getty Images.

Printed in the United States of America

Contents

How Penguins Migrate **4**

New Words **22**

Index **23**

About the Author **24**

Penguins live in the Southern **Hemisphere**.

They are birds. But they can't fly.

Penguins swim well.

They swim in cold water.

They live much of their lives in the sea.

7

Penguins **migrate**.

They move from one place to another.

9

Penguins raise their **chicks** in summer.

In winter, most penguins swim to warmer water to eat.

11

Emperor penguins are the largest penguins in the world.

They can be 4 feet (122 centimeters) tall.

Emperors migrate on land.

They move **inland** from the sea.

They walk or slide on the ice.

The female emperor lays an egg.

The male keeps it warm.

The female leaves to find food.

17

The female returns!

Her chick has hatched.

She feeds it.

The chicks return to the sea.

Someday they will come back.

They will raise their own chicks!

21

New Words

chicks (CHIX) Baby birds.

emperor (EM-per-er) A large penguin.

hemisphere (HEM-iss-feer) One-half of the world.

inland (IN-lend) Away from water.

migrate (MY-grate) To travel far.

Index

chicks, 10, 18, 20

egg, 16

emperor, 12, 14, 16

hatch, 18

hemisphere, 4

inland, 14

migrate, 8, 14

swim, 6, 10

About the Author

B.J. Best lives in Wisconsin with his wife and son. He has written several other books for children. He sees penguins at the zoo.

About

Bookworms help independent readers gain reading confidence through high-frequency words, simple sentences, and strong picture/text support. Each book explores a concept that helps children relate what they read to the world they live in.